YEARLING ∾

D1466650

YEARLING

Lo Kwa Mei-en

ALICE JAMES BOOKS
FARMINGTON, MAINE

10 9 8 7 6 5 4 3 2 1

Alice James Books are published
by Alice James Poetry Cooperative, Inc.,
an affiliate of the University of Maine at Farmington.

ALICE JAMES BOOKS
114 Prescott Street
Farmington, ME 04938
www.alicejamesbooks.org

Library of Congress Cataloging-in-Publication Data
Mei-en, Lo Kwa.
  [Poems. Selections]
  Yearling / Lo Kwa Mei-en.
      pages cm
  Includes bibliographical references and index.
  ISBN 978-1-938584-10-7 (pbk. : alk. paper)
  I. Title.
  PS3613.E42585Y43 2015
  811'.6--dc23

                            2014030174

Alice James Books gratefully acknowledges support from individual
donors, private foundations, the University of Maine at Farmington,
and the National Endowment for the Arts.

COVER ART: "Go Tell The Others" by Regan Rosburg, original artwork.

CONTENTS ᘒ

i.

ii.

iii.

ACKNOWLEDGMENTS ∾

This book owes a huge debt to my teachers and fellow students from the Creative Writing department of the Ohio State University who inspired me and inspired me to get to work. Thank you for the time I spent learning from you. Thank you to my family, near and far, for the support they have given me.

I am grateful to the editors of the following journals in which these poems previously appeared, some in different shape and form.

Anti-: "Tales of Burning Love"

Crazyhorse: "Addiction," "Ephemera," "Man O' War"

Cream City Review: "Left to Those I Love," "The Body with an Elegy inside of it"

CutBank: "The Currant"

Fairy Tale Review: "Pinnochia from Pleasure Island"

Guernica: "Taxi, Singapore, Ohio"

Gulf Coast: "Pinnochia, we loved you enough," "Pinnochia Sends Home the Manifesto," "Pinnochia on Fire," "Telegraph"

Hayden's Ferry Review: "Ariel," "Poem the Size of a Wing"

Indiana Review: "A Girl Thief's Illustrated Primer," "*Water,*
I want you"
inter/rupture: "Arrow"
Loaded Bicycle: "The Extinction Diaries: Psalm," "The Jubilee
Year of the Dead, inside of a Banyan Tree"
Nashville Review: "Self-portrait with a Teak Fleet of Sailing
Ships," "This Is Siren Country"
New Orleans Review: "Prodigal Animals"
Ninth Letter: "The Body That Has Something to Say"
PANK Magazine: "*hic sunt dracones,*" "Rough Husbandry,"
"Through a Glass through Which We Cannot See,"
"Yearling and Armor"
Sonora Review: "Reader, Fauna," "The Body as an Empty
Cup"
The Cincinnati Review: "Rara Avis Decoy"
The Kenyon Review: "*Canis lupus familiar song of songs*"
West Branch: "Canon with Wolves in the Water," "Era for
Drowning," "Era for Recovery"

"Era for Abandon" was featured in *Boston Review*'s online
2013 National Poetry Month feature.

This World is not Conclusion.
A Species stands beyond—

—Emily Dickinson

ARIEL

Temper, temper. More
of it: leather-lashed
to its own prow,

riding low. When battle
-ready, sober, I was gorgeous
in anger. Drop dead.

The hour swelled,
glassy, splitting
like a lip—then it was

done: one
devastation lent a hand
to the other.

I dreamt like a war machine
and woke like a child.

Through a Glass through Which
We Cannot See

ourselves, a dead star is the only luminary

around for years. We see it a temple, then
sack it. I needed something, so I sang it.

O my Jupiter, magnetic war-dreamer who still
swings by & low—I couldn't wear my red, red

storm on the bright outside for five hundred years.

I was a part, all surface, madly mirrored
across the world, just a stare, & kissing

back a false dreamer in the basement shrine.
The sofa would make no amends for being an altar.

The moon, too, had to be hauled up from there; once
now a needle, she tattooed the sweeping rib of

sky with the shape of a young woman's bark.

Once, I saw the alarming & cooled heart of myself,
the swallower & expert of damage but not of repair

in myself, & found new ways to give it all

away. Made a gun of two fingers & a thumb, jerked
to the throat, hunting & hunting & turning in the dark.

& O bright star of disaster, I have been lit.

ERA FOR DROWNING

Marvel by the morning, morning by the mile, mother,

I was not wise. Half-spill or honest, I drank the land down

the year it all got away from me. Yet yes I am all other

ways out all at once. I am half-spent and hell-bright as

the bad ones are, mother, a flicker deeper than the sea—

even that body I—mother, I drink so deeply always my

alas dawns slow. Hot little almost, *adieu*. Half always hawks

me back up, does the land I love but always a red-throated

rapture this way dives. Brutal my thermal drop. All bird

of burden, no prey. Not now. All day long *Doesn't want me*

back radios back to my reef from the era in which I lay

back down to die. But if new and electric in the deadened

of night becomes me, mother—but if all stars come extinct—

and when the salt of light falling in the water is all I see?

Taxi, Singapore, Ohio

Wife-beatered, bedroom burst with birds
and sons, my grandfather turns left on red

forever. We leave mainland for traffic or fish,
an island for snow, the hereditary list

to Away for his ghost taxi I never heard:
a quartet of poached songbird in the trunk.

In my mirror, I see the men I got drunk
off just breathing them, and tonight I wish

I took the well-trafficked kiss to market,
watched it sun and sell and darken

beside a silver moon of pomfret thanked
for flesh, for time. The fishmonger of me

walks home with a little fish a little empty,
but the next life will be landlocked, so we get

into a taxi and take somebody home
before that life surfaces: some snow, all stone

animals you cannot shoot, agreeable
species floated at the corners of yards.

We'll ghost into a life like minor chords,
make rearview eyes at what could have flown—

as a taxi turns left on red, four songs shut
in the trunk, testing the border like a cut

so open we'll know it forever, the words
that could have taken us home nowhere,

then brilliant, gone, fish sailing through air.

Self-portrait with a Teak Fleet of Sailing Ships

We were locked into the mystery
& wanted out. We moved like the half-great,

sea-chewed half girls on the old merchant prows,
so we didn't. Our backs were screwed to

one great thing, to the great by then
ruth that canaried through the ruthless bodies

of water, while everything we had above the waist
ran & outran the vessel we could not run

ourselves off. After midnight cast its lot
we cast about with our elemental heads

for a requiem shark, disaster, its undertow
& drag. We were after the

hot knife & compass of the flesh. We would have
drowned ourselves in it, if. Sailors'

stars bandaged our foreheads with light as if they,
too, longed for arms' breach. When what we'd been told

was enough, was enough
to abandon, get by, abandon, & barely arrive.

Poem the Size of a Wing

To think, so many have never found another
at least
as sick as they are.

In sleep, I do not dream without anger
stroking at the soft pit of my knee.

And your French saying sounds like a licked stamp
riding its bad news—

china saucer over the wall socket, breaker
and thing to break, thing of beauty

waiting to be comprehended, as you do not wait

for me. For that—the pathetic bolting
the tail of the question mark
to what I've already lost, and the thought

-provoked past, sutured, stuffed up with gardeners

walking away from the gardens.
Next door, a moon-bellied bat surfs the horizon

down to its domestic grove, and it will
have to do.

They who have not seen these things
say, *The young man had something inside him*

and it led him to all crimes—
and then they, spinning, take a finger,

train it on the wobbling, black magnet in my chest.

All summer, there's a loud blooming
of reddish weeds by the roadside. There's a city
that road-forces its way through
for the thought grown within me

calling, *The city fears for me*, and after that,
I feared the city. There's this thin honesty.

It gives itself up like a birthmark the size of a wing,
size of a sadness, of a thing of beauty

that covers the face I am touching.

DEVIL OF DEFIANCE

"There are three things that are never satisfied, yea, four things say
not, It is enough: The grave; and the barren womb; the earth that
is not filled with water; and the fire that saith not, It is enough."

—*Proverbs 30:15-16, King James Version*

If I can't have you I will say *Enough*, never. I swear,
to speak of you, words gather and slam back, black
        -lit, the wing lifted off the spine of every sea—every

red latitude leads back to you. How I swore to live
        alone if I had to, unflocked, arcana, a murder out for
scrap, watching that wave slice into sweet shoulders

of sand. I can't live for summer another day but for
you and I will not, will not—prey for me, dolls cut
        out of me, dazed in a canopy, star-mouths in metallic

clay, run over in the yard. Merely, they lie there on
        tiny backs of defeated fabric, the want of breakable
skin a sign of what breaks. How welcome your hell

        -bound hand unclothing the lines. How profanely
gorgeous its scar by blaze. Else my own confesses it's
        for you, of you, hurting every word I never. Else just

say it, *Let there be bone*, and I'll break, let there be
        light, I could be, let me be the fourth thing, and yes I
swear. What I wanted makes me want you faster. My

name is under earth, its hot, cracking throat, where
nowhere I run with you could turn me into ashes fast
enough to keep you. Never—and I the third thing,

undone like the mane of god and wanting for flood.
Ever you are the first thing. Heaven shut, and I knew
more than a heart could say. Say my heart madly

beneath yours. Now say my name till saying kills. Now
break, break. And throw me down on bales of bold
earth, where all that burns is never, and ever, enough.

Becoming Radio

Hello, hello—have I ever lived with a need

that went up to echo in the summer
attic of the throat? Or I'm just beating, just a slow

wing staked between the signal and the noise
of what goes to ground to report. Spring broke

down in the lap of its mother since she
won't come around. I thought myself ready,

restless in the register of hips and eyes. This is
an emergency. This is an epilogue that began

there, a static rain of violence. Hello,
I made myself look as loud as you are,

radio. I rode a quick equation and breathed
like shipwreck on its way up, sounding off

echoes per inch of sunlight rediscovered. I found
the terror of saying when I could have sung.

Radio, I'm just beating, just a dirty,
slow wing. On air, I can't shut up, listen

much. I'm just my own interruption.

Rough Husbandry

After you, I begin at the Natal plum:

a babe with one hand
stuck in the terracotta *O* of my first jaw.

When I bite back, the garden grows back. Then
everything does.

The red eye-fruit of the mirabelle
tree does and I watch the tiny pome

hang itself, determined, bloody bell.

A wasp drags its breast up the wall
of the stink-sweet pitcher,

stuffed, half-taxidermied by lust.
Mimosa touches herself beneath a tree—

and you, still everywhere, slight pollen.

One thing races itself against its time
and then another, but like a pale twin,

I keep my hand on the throat of every small death.
I scream when *Carnosa compacta* cannot,

think, *Don't come back.* I do my best

to mean it, stripped down beneath the Hindu Rope
vine. I'll be moving like a girl's loose dread

-lock, like a cane of Wasted Ophelia, rocked
at the root in a bower of weeds.

THE EXTINCTION DIARIES: PSALM

The world is another cage I cannot map. Once
emptied, the ocean will sit down, a love song inside it:
a black fish mouthing *Hallelujah* to the walls, opening
itself on them for good. Glory being, beloved,

our mane was dynamite. We fell asleep with a jet
strand swallowed and for life couldn't light it. Not like
a gun in the hand. The lands of what cannot illumine
grow deep and a mouth roots then uproots like an

ant-engined hill. Nothing eats. To know what once could
is to know why. No river shatters past as fed as a city
of straight lines and no tender enters the fault
of our body. From its deeps, the white coin of vertebrae

in a bowl of hips tells the future. May the meek inherit
something gorgeous. May I. May a geography of
defiant climes shock the ocean's flesh, its fish many
thunders—may they ring true. May we. May

I run in our sleep, keeping up and more with kings
too great to see in the dark. Too great to see grow
the tides, each made in the image of a shut door.
Behind, god, a school of tongues, singing the keys.

THE BODY AS AN EMPTY CUP

They bring things to you in smaller glasses
when they are stronger. Rogue hazelnut

ale, well-diluted soap, blush wine: these are not
stronger things so should come in buckets. Yes,

I see what you see—girl all appetite
riddled with holes. No, my throat has not drunk

down a barrel of Dawn. The West Coast sky
says I should've expected that from you.

So it comes down to forecasts and delays.
We used to sit, stare, and wait for what

was promised. When buckets of weaker
copies came instead, I recited *cardamom*,

whiskey, blow beneath my breath. If I ever
come back to you, it will be in thimbles.

Pinnochia, we loved you enough

to dream up a simple boat that could, with confidence,
slice through a continent's wet shelf for new gold and
other precious curios, and then we put you in it, dear
thing, but not before a real hand came down to carve

the map of worldly want into your brow, so you may
but look overboard, once lost, to know your place.
We will imagine you, unsinkable girl, stirring the seas
from *Tsae* to *Tsew*, and the sea sniffing at the cherry

notes of your bones, of the fresh wound of your head,
a daydream of something like blood as you row and
row for days. Pinnochia, you have been loved. Hard,
unsaying hips and tongue, you are indelible, we love

you that much. We dreamed a shark's awl of a face
and mechanical thrust, dreamed the dream of you, half
-in, half-out of his throat. So the hand came down kind
and sanded your breasts away for speed, for seconds

you, half-in, half-out of a devil, must cast yourself
away. Pinnochia, we could not bear to see you
destructed even in our sleep. Pinnochia, you will never
die. We bless you, living ghost of treasure, imagined

back into coffers wide enough for you to sleep in,
the half-sweet smell of you radiating from the walls.
There you will intuit all things done for a reason, so
you will do great things, we know, as the hand comes

down into your legs, making of two things one, brief
tableaus of hind-light, spine, and blue, green, blue run
through the mind of the hand as he gives you the body
that can outrun the tides, and so we deliver you

into the oceanic womb, half girl, new beast, and you will
go forth, reborn in the image of how we loved you: like
a bride, Pinnochia, like a thousand golden fish in the sea,
alive in the mouth of the coffer, the realest thing for days.

A Girl Thief's Illustrated Primer

To guarantee safety, go back inside and count
to noon. To make honey by honest trees,
press for time. Either way, all numbers are hellhound
as well as holy, but what did you expect?

A little divine torture has always been
the way in, and waiting for daylight
robbery won't leave you deadly. Or, take my
word away and light up the teeth in the tumbler

all at once, like the locked door is a yawning
god and you the very last *Alleluia*—
at once, as if your heart shredded its school skirt
and shotgunned over the yard for home.

Be need with a black glove riding the wrist.
Be first-felony Eve in the red telephone booth
outside the garden, a battle coal
dialing herself back into the war.

They kept you on the wrong side all along.
Hold a tension wrench closer. Treat your gates
like they were lovers and listen for the *Yes*.
And there it is, but look at what you found inside.

Ephemera

This was the room that held me like a grave.
That was the bad dream taking off its boots

and button words. So long,

coyote-dotted June and zodiac cave
where I fractured and wheeled. The carrion

flies fall away, unsung.

I hope their children wander
more freely than we have, though not,

necessarily, into our bodies.

Body, gabion, lit
cage of copper skin and threaded blood:

you'll know one more death, as you knew you would.

I'll puncture through, the hook
in you, though barely.

This time, a hare will flood out from the fox
warren of me, though its knees knock
and the stars slouch like fat coins in the mud.

It will burn softly, proudly, for leaving

no sign of passage. This floods like a sail
-shaped ear. Watch me press it to the wall.

hic sunt dracones

In the country of your childhood, country of the crossroad, of the

winged creature at the hour of its extinction, you put a secret in the ground

to kill the secret and the ground goes black. Now the ground is buried

by blank snow, your mercenary name, and the strange, red swell of a barn

swallow's belly, deranged by a bracelet of teeth: all thoughts you thought desire

erased through its existence. The starved months wheel overhead,

weightless like a map that carries no weight but the country that tattoos it,

and as truthful. They know that the sun rides over the rider of all fantastic

beasts that surge to their world's edge. They lie and wait, for you

are not the rider. You run riddled by the wide knife of your old name

and the snow of the country swallows the sounds it made.
The swallow

goes black. The germ bucks up through the black. O germ in
the frantic

husk of the feeling body. Beware. It's war. Unfold. You learn
fire and fire

learns you. It has followed you here before. It feeds you
through

the year like a jet skein of mane through an original fist and
chariots

from the canopy to snow to belly to black to the edge of
your name.

Tongues of ash break off small bites of the map and its body.
What's left

calls itself firstborn, final leg, lone backbone the length of an
arrow

shot, the mark flown, a badland, fauna played out in the
dark.

The Jubilee Year of the Dead,
inside of a Banyan Tree

The underworld is what you thought it'd be,
but not where. We who know not what we are
tick the record of animal loss off our fingers.
We give names to the faces: *badger; black canary;*

physical alarm now a lantern. We who will die
more than once bellow about. *Oh my monarch.*
Crocodile dear, dear, dear. The branches craze
with memory's fauna, for a time, and no

friend or last lover comes back to be faced
and renamed, but that was life. *Termite queen,*
you tunnel my heart. You've still got your
self upon you, song stuck to creature, a fact to

get used to in the year of jubilee and the dead.
You will wear it like a harness of wings of roots.
You're like banyans, more stranger than strangler:
you could breathe without burying. *Orca, orca,*

was that you? Oh phoenix. Come brighten. Wade
in the year of your acre and flood, a mere, lit fig
hung from your neck to lantern you back and forth
to a place where we will speak your name again.

Meaning no more hooks. Mean it. Not in me nor you. Though

what whaled beneath whales on on my wave. Meaning no more

soaks a skin it needed to get through this or, honest, get through.

To you. As I weathered at a you. Meaning lets you let down me

as anchor to the floor, but when no tether, friendly fix, or fire

contained did hold me I sank that line from my horizontal low.

But this. If my bite turns tail, my net full zero, how will I kill

all the what of what bittered my bent to the end? Won't better

come at me better, or just you come back? Know me harder:

all that mean took a bait out of me. A skim of red what scans

what beasts below a wave bigger than us at all. Battle means my

reward inherent by now so how won't I kill the prize is what

kills me. My means cut lines last seen in the wild. I mean what I

slay. No more hooks, I say, for sake of my body. Forsake your

great white body. Or our throat, the need for breath. I mean it.

THE BODY WITH AN ELEGY INSIDE OF IT

In time, we'll lose another page's worth
of what made the missive figs grow
fat as a love word rounding a lip and finite
as the body addressed. No matter

how hard. If your name has lodged
like a sickle beak in a fist-body of fruit,
what do I answer to. I'm awake and a vehicle,
though not readily. I know because

what's inside me takes off. How light
will my bones get, down in the plot, and
what company will they learn to keep.
Where will you be. Look, how morning's

strange birds freak and stain like a smashed cup.
It's a mourner's reversal, and the dark just
pours up. See what's left to see in this hollow,
it says, naming itself, nodding, refusing

to sleep. Or release. Or come home.

Pinnochia from Pleasure Island

Now I think of what I'd die to forget. Now I forget.
    Where did I grow up, get out—was I as rich as a golden
yolk waiting to crack in the hay? Where I come from
    would I go back? If yes, reload me. And if yes, accident,
but nobody can brave enough to see we're just buck
    -shot spat from out the mouth of a motherland. So, bang,

wet me like a tooth with a wicked root. We're target
    far from being dear for long. Now you make me dress
the wound I turned myself into when I bit into two.
    Now you might get up inside it and show me the whip
-stitch anew, or finger-test my tourniquet, bandwidth
    on top of me, make me shake like a head. Now you like

to know my real name, what to say yet louder when
    on the outside for good. What's not good you can't get
out of a corset fast enough, here, and I came unlaced
    fast-paced. My body's a dress (cut from a fond hell I tore
off the tongue of the real), a first name for what's beneath.

Now the word for *intake* is that for *swallow*, smallest
    beast licking its way down the sky once like lightning.
Because here, somebody can open their mouth wider
    yet. Laws don't break here. It's like I can still break
because here, somebody wants to open my mouth, wide
    beast licking its way down the sky once, like lightning.

Now the word for *intake* is that for *swallow* (smallest
    of the tongues of what's real), first name for the thing
    beneath,

fast-paced. My body's a dress. Cut from fond hell, I tore
out of the corset fast. Enough, here, and I come unlaced
on the outside for good, not what's good. You don't get
to know my real name, what to say and louder yet when

on top of me, making me shake like a head. You're like
a new stitch, my finger-tested tourniquet, its bandwidth.
Now you might get up inside it. So show me the whip,
the wound I turn myself in to when I bite into two, too
far from being dear. Now you make me dress. So long.
Whet me like a tooth with a wicked root. I am target

shot, spat out from the mouth of a mother. So, bang,
but nobody can be brave enough to see I'm just bucked.
Would I go back? If yes, reload me. If yes, accident,
yolk waiting to crack in the hay. Where I come from,
where did I get out? Was I richly young and golden?
Now, I think of what I'd die to forget.

Prodigal Animals

Let the low tides unbutton themselves about our feet
in plain sight of all. There's a word for where they go
meaning *years* to an animal with a softer spine and inner
ear. Meaning a minor world, emergent, its language mine,
still scarred by echoes and oil. The nights I tried to know this,
to measure a broken muscle by the wing it now resembles,
a knife by anything but its history. I counted out silence in
revolutions and lost not all—each exhalation an open book
of matches and every vowel you heard an heirloom flag.
There are other words for the places I have gone indelibly.
A kinder geographer would unstitch names from borders,
dismantle the legends and maps. Cradle me with needle teeth
and sight the old invasive species when you wake. Chokecherry's
bark at my tongue like a bullet. Dawn starts like a bullet
but from here we signal and net one sun from the watery
distances, taking time, so moved by its twin in the dissonant,
reddish sky. Here, I suspect we would survive on nothing
thicker than switchblades of grass. If not for long, still,
we would. This is my nocturnal face, unnatural
steel sweeping its hot tides. There's one word for that aftermath.
Let its light wash out and through, a nova unlocking a rib cage.
Other animals navigate in absolute darkness, taking shape
at the end of a minor world, for which we have no word.

ADDICTION

What weather. What muscular

weather domesticates a woman
like a key and tin sparrow.

And does a machine call that bird *Mine*.

What splinter is clutched for days between its feet.

What water turns its tiny back
to rust and which lake

does it name its metal throat after,
does it see

a cage that swallowed others' bodies like wet seed.

When do we go back for what
we came for,

and what half
-broken strap of weather holds itself up,

like a blindfold, to the shuddering
vein of horizon, for

one thing to fly, suddenly
singing, beneath it.

ARROW

Drawn, uninvited, I'm an animal with a price on her head,

wrecking a bed of wet pine: I steal through the field twice:

as long as the day is a shot yard of light, let me scope you,

darling on a notch, lonely eye painted red in the low dark

marking me. Stalked, my body's a dictionary of only chances.

A dame is what's fantastic, alter dam who never had to do

without. A dress is good to lift. Hard twang, dumb arch,

one body here knows well: a quiver is a dream of being held

about the middle by a mouth of handsome leather. Abetted

and moving mark, needle moved: let fly. I hound my own

neck these days, but spring means something with a wingspan

so dark as my dark hurtles past itself, as you do. If you

could take wing, shake the hand, would—? Little quarrel, listen.

A kill is what the heart calls its instrument hurrying on home.

Left to Those I Love

To the geese: every egg the neighbor shook
as you slept. The bones and balls and chords
to hiss: *Get off me, fucker.* Freedom.
Freedom. For my very first executioner:

a searing blade of grass, an open eye. Just
once. To Christ and our father: our last night
together, on my knees until sunup. Sometimes I
miss that. Eight years' penitence and rue

(which I seem to have paid elsewhere).
To Elia: our children, their children. *Nyet.*
I don't want to carry them any longer.
I unleash the lot of us into the arcana

beside the unforgivable: my tiny pot of war
paint, my old masters, the sunflowers
yawning wild through the open window
as a train discards one country for the next.

The blueprint, to no one, that caught
the blow of the wind and bolted off with
what was promised me—a little loss, and
at some point, levitation.

Tales of Burning Love

—Louise Erdrich

O boy! Stand on one foot until the good weather
changes. Now on the other, a season of yellowing
weeds between the teeth of every sidewalk. *A sign
of lone resilience*, a voice will say, but nobody here
can read if it means having to know the future.
Go to all fours and run, don't walk. Use your thumbs.
In the reddest room, someone else can be your
Christ for once, a lick of salt in an undrinkable sea.
Or, your Thoreauvian beetle, mapping the border and
natural law of a stranger's bathtub. Who washes whom
unclothed, crouched over a fragrant, grassy bar
as infant territory—a whole world—is midwifed by he
who maps the land, somewhat wild and marked
by flag and ink, is who writes the letter nobody can read.
This one was scrolling over the sheets like cloud cover.
Somebody in the room could tell a story and end it
clean as a house sprouted up between fences, between
the loves you up and race to through the old field. Get up
on the roof. Up to your clean neck. Up on your own
two hands, feet washing the stars. Just say them.

Water, I want you

fixed like a double Scorpio, sworn to the red
star phase of Fahrenheit. Run, run

your body down my body, and be brave.
Be everywhere. What I know of forever

is that it is not real, not mine, but you
could teach me a thing or two. It's about time

I showed you what I am not, what I could be.
When I eat a little of my own heart in the Ohio

valley morning and it grows back on a beach
across the Pacific like a new state flower,

I say that *I am filled with something*
that resembles you. I say, *Be mine,*

every time, but I know the shape that leaving
takes, half-loverly, half god.

When half-dead, I take you in my mouth
and you steam into speech. You say, *Descend,*

little chord, throw yourself from the sky
in a stream of piss and vinegar and holy

fallout. Sometimes, when I cannot help but know
I will die, I feel the grave shovel-sutured shut

over my mouth—wait and wait for my very first rain.
It's official as a sip of blood. I want your body

and your birthright. I must wander. Be brave. Rise
elsewhere.

Era for Abandon

And the sea wave, wasted on its want, too, takes the method

home and crashes against. Lifelike, I waste, too. My hit comes

again and the green breath breaks against as for rock leaping at

and far beyond the surface, its wet fiction, the facts of fracture

mere seed locked down in the wave. O well with a false bottom,

no, pit, undrinkable, I drink from you and dawn to find I drank.

I am no current but a bolt. This time I will exit myself, sure, but

then again I wonder through a valley with an exit sign every time.

My hit comes again and the jealous breath breaks. My hell comes

again and again and against. That old edge. Like breathing so life

-like breath wastes itself over me. There was a time the tremor

came and halved the vane it struck with a love like a bell that rang

to the body of the sea. There was that jolt. But I'm no current but

a volt and chain. And control, that thing with a hull with a hole.

The Currant

Now come the thought of a blood-filled bell.
Now come a rude well of air; mineral blush on the prairie.
Now come the bat, flown scrap of patience, slung through
my door for light, destructive as a small god. We're deep with small
accidents. The hand I adore
flies through a closed window for love. Not for me
are pale candles pooled on the floors of the carnival gourds.
Not for anybody could a clean shape burn through them.
Frost clocks the sky. One forecast, quiet as the gray pearl
of a pigeon's breast, descends to a wire fence and grows
fat for our hurts. One forecast gleams, but a flock of them is
as common as weapons we took to ourselves and had
taken to us. What hour can we ask to shepherd us in, so thin,
clownish with a scar and others? We who dream the freak
currants of November, dream the high tides,
the final map of a body lost at last, touch them and go
blind as the chain link eyes of the fence. The hand
I adore wades through the red, raptured currants.
I dream I will never shut my eyes again, and this time
I can see it. I heard a bell through blood.

III ∾

*Feed this to the neighborhood. To the neighborhood dogs
in heat*, I say, the smallish stars hunting what the slow stars
unscrewed. They streak. They eat all the gravity on the block
& I bring it back. When I'm got, when she's good, the omega
bitch rises up like a gorgeous, violet weed. She runs high like
an arrow unleashed. She takes her tail in her mouth. Accomplice
stars gnaw on the dark. This is how we want to make love out
at the fence—in fat grass, a hound at our back, knees rocked
& boxing a dent under a belled, red alarm of alien honeysuckle,
bodies folding out until huge fogs & landscapes that spell *I, I,
I was prepared to die*. So feed this to something fast. Pick me.
Down in the wings a hunting body paces like black honey &
I go down. This is how we want to feel against the cellar wall.
Once I died, in morning. But one thing composted. It was this.
So female weeds upset the asphalt like a broken wine, & wild
dogs butchered my heart & fled before it blew. They felt good
like god, like the body & its sex, forever pushing each other's
heads down in the wave of heaven. Like hot milk, winter fruit,
gift of the magi, a mother's white, Holocene breath. Some heavy
stars submit: down the street, to a planet's core, unbelievably
quick. You needn't feed yourself for nights like this. Can't you
see. My heart's a hotel & it's full with hounds. At your poor
neck my alpha & omega will leave open a gospel of teeth. Last
book. First page. A red illumination to light the animal amen.

Yearling and Armor

I am here, at last, dressed in plain mustard and tiger,
carrying on with my fake claw and faulty calendar,
the old fetishes—spit and spice and sea—loaded
behind my teeth. Another year, another armor,

though I was told otherwise. Another way of speaking:
What if the body had been a spell and the confidant broke it.
Or a city, half-woken, and my comrade blazed it. Inside,
a voice prays for the bantam mouthing off at the anti-dawn

to silence or become other, entirely: firebird
feeding off ash, or a photograph of somebody
brave. What if my face had been a sign so I painted it,
time's direction rolling back and back like a maiden's

domesticating spine, and what the body had in store
for itself—potential seeds and starry cloves stacking the inner
shelf—was pulled into the mouth of the ocean. So on,
another city, new, almost. What if I knew I would pay

all for entrance, to be entranced, or else to almost
always be. And if I let hot ritual wrap its arms about me.
Then another, and another. And felt the body move again
like a mouthful of sea, or a yearling in the armory.

Rara Avis Decoy

> "You simply take a piece of wood and cut out everything
> that doesn't look like a duck."
>
> —*Currituck Sound carver*

Call me darling on the surface.
Call me honey of the sound

all my fathers make as they welt
the skin of the lake. My name is hooded

diver on a string, little Red Head bastard.
I call my mothers down to eat without a sound.

They beat, beat, slant to water and stitch
feet to the reflection of feet. I'm a favorite

child of the gouge and the knife, the human
hand that makes a collar about the ruby

neck of my father. He and my other fathers
drove down through shallows like drill bits

and they came up silver. My name is the spoils
of thin flesh, the minnow's salt eye

plucked clean for a mother. Call me game
over. Wild diamond rocking on the floor

of a predatory boat. Point and say *sweet traitor*
to the wood and water for wanting to be made

of both. My name is I know not what I am
as a country of mothers and fathers comes down.

They call me sleeping beauty. I dream I am
in flight, body unfolding, folding, a bullet

wounding water again and again—the mysterious
love of a father and mother a two-barreled

gaze. The gun in my dream speaks my name
and sees a beating vein. Takes aim—

Pinnochia Sends Home the Manifesto

When I'm august I will wear you like a cat fur coat.
      The smallest leather in the world. Like now, nothing
heavy will get in or out the eyes but you, you off a
      chain. Now I'm so hard like a hand of coal you have
to a count of three. Three. Roll that eye right on
      up, naked as my birthday. Long as we're slanting,
how's this real eyeful for an eyeful? Yesterday
      I'll give birth to a real ass by holy syndicate light.
He will turn me to flash kindling under the light
      and we'll bray together, on three, so bloodless,
the most terrific virgin in the world and also god
      knows what. All night long I wore me like a glass
in the wall, for looking not in nor out at the house.
      I did interpret all gifts for worse or worse, my god
sign, sick mother, no cocktail real enough for this.
      My high is a false high; I'm the prophecy going right
through me. My god is god of wraths and unease.
      My son will take me off like a rocket's skirt and take
off for hay and lake runoff on all fours, and my fist
      will slide, a hot, new arrow right under the righteous
head of god, or whomever, I care not I cannot, and he
      will want to die and I will make him sing for what
I used to sing. You could baptize a battlefield in it. And
      walk walk walk away. When I'm a march, crows will
spear you up like a fish on legs, throw you into my
      arms, a neat bowl of blood. I birth babes not born
of blood exactly, so they cry. They are my smallest
      sunrise in the galaxy, amen. All night long I scratch

the unforgiving skins in my head. I suture the sails
        of a fucked boat. For love, I'd eat this planet up to
get us to the next. But for the sake of leather, I'll polish
        off nothing before daybreak but for you.

Catch you in the back room playing Mother.
Catch you like ghosts. Let you go again.
Let you grow tall & gold in the wild holly for
a little information on how to get close. Stop.
You need this. Send you brother, okay cowboy,
bad weather friend. Send rain. Left left tattoo for lover.
Something to hurt alongside in the tender acre.
Can you keep that up for long. Stop. Stop. See
I am daughter writes a last letter. Left the parakeet
alongside in fine cage. Shows you how pretty I am
not so I stuck a wing in each fist & rode. X
out. Dirty words of my dowry. Also out. Drum a
short rain to let me know you get there okay.
Catch you here maybe. A streak of moss up for sun
& the minute oranges & call them clementine. Thanks
you in summer. Stop. Got me. Can send more sweet
orbs if you think so. Tomorrow is nothing could last
forever day. Stop. Dash. Stop. See I pack a bag. See
I catch you on the road gotten dark. Send moon.
Stop. Send short & long rain to invite & comfort
expedition. Can't make the map you say if I try. & I try
everything. Even ink. Even ink. Even both.

This Is Siren Country

"...whose bodies are unnamed but whose songs..."
—Nancy S. Love, "Why do the Sirens Sing?"

Once you were as empty as a wind-filled sail,
but you'll never fall asleep again. You are welcome.

All summer, the sun is bolted to a red wheel. It breaks
through a cloud's belly, radiant, surgical, salt

nets spreading on every man's shoulder. It is so good
everybody lies down. Nobody rests. All say *Hail*

to roots of my flesh, this weather to die for. Come and go
in the bedrooms like water, the old sleeplessness of

a body's red sky—signal after signal plays off skin,
rounds the corner of a knee, all pupils lit from behind

as a morning. Soon we set a calendar of bacchanals.
We set a pace we cannot follow and we follow once

again starved. Again a sigil that starts in the marrow.
Again a nameless daughter, sampling the black stripe

on a roasted tongue, velvet and severe. Again speech.
Hail to every body, swollen as a sail, tied in knots.

And hail to the mother and father you never knew
we had. To you, no generation walked on water

before us, so we sing down the family tree and cast
original seed. We are armada. We are cannon. You

are in a land of mythic passage, where want comes
to pass as real. Believe it like a christ, a cross—

This is called a harbor. This is a safe
that won't sink with your secret into a wet bed.

The past cannot touch you. O hail your harvest gaze.
Love, the great butcher, kept us flesh as hell, diving

for dark terrain, but who can swim with open arms?
It is good to be unafraid of death, we say, crawling

high through a hot wave of weeds. Come, we swear
you will rise in fields again, ears raw, burst with grain.

The Second Flowering of the Mammals

all the ocean warming it's a good mouth all of the good hunters
grow large & then so do the prey even to the feet as if the better

to be followed to get hot & fodder or no to flee & the feet are
to lead you the fauna wickedness of water with its lunar brine &

yes to tease you with with a way down & even better the night
we keep the other warm & by running is no excuse for running

in a line feet that would survive in front & feet that would eat
behind fleeing what won't survive back off the earth we shed

oxygen like a leash we full tilt until a planetary dawn we dawn
throttle so that a throat is a threat & thus a feast takes two

one to give thanks one to see a god out of chase or chase
the endless the endless & the less we serve a hunger larger

than us than itself & having survived the good god sea it could
know better but hunger won't stay down in the wet hunger

started wet & like a winter of a giant sun & system so famine
so flood so summer so the hunters grow hunger & so do a

lot of us & what will outlive the years of gold & harvest we
let it go we love it we run it & down we go together empty

THE BODY THAT HAS SOMETHING TO SAY

For centuries—reports that left-handedness
is all wrong. Doctors with their skull auger and bowl
      and mother tongues everywhere
      have things to say about: the instinctual

dominance that splits a body in half;
which side of a girl reigns the darker.
      The bolder? The I will never kneel
before your fire. And
               oh, what mulish fire.

If you touch a stem of rosemary to its little, blue
core the truth snakes itself out
      in a thin-lipped guffaw of smoke.
      Namely: the habit

of sucking limes, spare use of sesame oil. How
the father-in-law did or did not mean it
when he called his son's wife
      Crooked Path.

But over all confessions, this

subversion—a salted trick that's had leaders
of men seeing the body in fractions
      like land.

It was never a question of one side
over the other. The body that has something to say

knows better than that.
    Lights everything on fire with one hand
    and tends coals with the other.

READER, FAUNA

It's a zoo in here, & it's so hard to exist
on the same side of the glass as you.

For so long I've been Lady Panthera the half-dead

boxing cat on good days, & gone gypsy
moth shooting the breeze with its body, with

Blackbird Blue Note, on the worst. For so long
I've wanted to join you up on the treble clef.

I don't want to keep my half note lonely in hell

so I asked you to come along. I wouldn't ask you
any place you had not emerged from, already,

but I can't blame you for not wanting to go back.
So expect to be invited to other, auroral

sierras & haunts, where we'll scar both star
-studded knees kneeling on a red

blade of the electro-heavens. Bring your
own empty bottles. We'll yoke

the necks to a little solar wind & let the message go.

This is how a cloud watches itself.
This is dancing over wild Yukon with my skeleton

on the outside. Now you try. Name the creature
you saw birthing through the hell-cloud, &

name the note that could have slaughtered it.

Man O' War

—*November 1, 1947*

Before a field locks its horizon in place. A martial
claw of cardinals freckles the sky half-red. Before

a sea change can bolt the chambers of your sixteen
-handed heart. The ghost of long grasses is hauling

behind it a blanket of perennial trophy. The meadow
ghost is so deep it turns itself out. Before the god

of the wild miles, of gorgeous and brutal unshod
grace can come for you, her flank as high as yours

and burning higher than the fires of photographic
light. Bulbs of velvet gold wink in the insect

night like meteors sailing, each mate a larval ocean
tossing beneath the constellation like your head

in a hold. The ghost of plateau says even the
chestnut blade of your face was, once, dirt of a star,

a bold specimen from a giant long gone. Before
the females feed knowing in the fields, unparallel

gods, early ghosts, slipping into dawn. You are old—
you slid into the stalls like a beloved bullet, and

then out. *Out, out*, a muddy sparrow brightly
spat at you who will head stunning sons in what

nobody calls a circle. Nobody buys a singular loss
can saddle you to the knees. Before the god of war

you kneel in blown Kentucky blue, she a trigger, she
a color of dove, of endless miles, her skull a moon

outstretched. Her nostrils at your neck bleed two hot
banners of breath. The grass sweats gold. Fences turn

to ghosts of mythic cost, padlocks for eyes. Before
your ghost can see right through them. A report of

wings leaps from the long sea of dawn and the god
goes off.

ERA FOR RECOVERY

If a matter of choice then my choir, surely. If voices

then pitchfork. Then just choose, if choosing is just

or barely. Confess: if my breast is a bird at his glass

the room is just a good cage with less window.

So breaking, interring. If bird, bust. So forgetting, allowing,

then burying. That seems—but then, no wake in sight

equates. If a machine of choice then the marvel of it

all about moved on at great speed and no accelerando

to choose or confess: if with it, confessor, then for me

forsake me. And if old god as given then offer or get off.

Choral echoes in a cage imply when lock then release

when and if one is ready. But then believers in no one

make a critical mass. I mean matter. As if trying to can't

collar. It was a master of choice. I could have kneeled.

Pinnochia on Fire

There is a line that could make you love me really,
        but reeling, I spend the words like virgin coin for
a real girl on the line. When things got bad, starlight

        began to prick. So I kept the sky returnable,
sad wheel. My arm the Mayday flare, leg a picnic's
        pyro dahlia—when I go up I'll keep my head on

a pillow when I can, see back to sea, say a syllable
        is a hook. And the word for my wick of a tongue
you'll find between my teeth. You want me ultra

        -lingual, ready-maid, but I'm a match head to head
in the gutter, and the gutter creaks above the main
        avenue of heaven. I kept myself bony dry, a sugar

cube of vermouth: I cut myself by the grain, cool
        and slender as a fuse with a sister; I missed her over
over over like a bullet train shooting past myself

        through the tunnel of a broken bone, and on time,
not mine. But I light up like an obscene October
        sky celebrating a stroke of war. When all still burns

from all I see, the taste of ash a horny flower on
        a hard female tongue, say *holiday*. Say *harvest*. Stay
back. Stand back, trigger this. I'll keep it real, go

hurt something to love it, real, good, find the center
of aurora in me, the second of ignition. Hothouse
        flower scheming the hole of the firework, I'll hurt

to keep wild tonight. A sky for my savage cross
        -haired wheeling under; a field of soon cooled stars—
temperature and light, so hot, so real, I come alive.

Canon with Wolves in the Water

The world may end in fire. My Holocene repeats.
My love of horrid thaw recycles back the year I
repeat only myself, mad as infant ferns or fracture

in a face of tidal ice. Wolves fall from the middle
of the era like water off a wave of ice. I, lupine
dam of lowest loss, crouch to eye its low waves

for years to come. Came hell or high. Came kin
hard swept to sea by a year of rain. Come withhold
what was left inside me. You, fang half sank

like news of good or evil in the skin of the thinning,
feral year, or your dream of dying repeated.
You or I descend from the first bayou of good or

worse, unclearing the water under sky. I was and
was a pelt on fire and under it, everything we had
had been had. The world may end in fire. Or

how I watch the water is wolves treading water
for life. How a wolf watching water is how I want
how I want to love the new apocalypse for good.

R E C E N T   T I T L E S   F R O M   ∽
A L I C E   J A M E S   B O O K S

Alice James Books has been publishing poetry since 1973. The press was founded in Boston, Massachusetts as a cooperative wherein authors performed the day-to-day undertakings of the press. This collaborative element remains viable even today, as authors who publish with the press are also invited to become members of the editorial board and participate in editorial decisions at the press. The editorial board selects manuscripts for publication via the press's annual, national competition, the Alice James Award. Alice James Books seeks to support women writers and was named for Alice James, sister to William and Henry, whose extraordinary gift for writing went unrecognized during her lifetime.

Designed by Dede Cummings

Printed by Thomson-Shore